From Salisbury
To Romsey
River Test
To Romsey
Bramshaw
Brook
Cadnam
Canterton
Castle Malwood
Bartley
Totton
Station
Redbridge
Eling
Station
SOUTHAMPTON
River Itchen
Lyndhurst Road Station
New Forest Union
FOREST BOUNDARY
Longdown
Ashurst Lodge
Marchwood
Emery Down
Bolton's Bench
LYNDHURST
Dibden
SOUTHAMPTON WATER
Netley Abbey
Hythe
Black Down
New Park
Queens Bower Wood
Balmer Lawn
SOUTHAMPTON AND DORCHESTER LINE
Beaulieu Heath
Fawley
Brockenhurst
Station
Brockenhurst Park
Beaulieu
River Exe
Hatchet Pond
Langley
Bottom
RAILWAY
Latchmoor Pond
Lymington River
Marlpit Oak
Lymington or Beaulieu Heath
Boldre
Dark Water
Exbury
Lepe
St. Leonards
Needs Ore Point
LYMINGTON BRANCH
Sowley Pond
FOREST BOUNDARY
Station
LYMINGTON
Pitts Deep
THE SOLENT

Pollards, People and Ponies

Frederick Golden Short

Pollards People & Ponies

Mike Walford

Published by Short Publications, Pickwick, Corsham, Wiltshire

First published July 1979 by Short Publications

ISBN No. 0 906823 00 5

Photoset in 11pt Century Schoolbook at Chippenham Typesetting, Wiltshire

Film, origination and plates by Sayl Reproductions of Southampton

Text paper - Nimrod Cartridge 100 gsm supplied by Link Paper Sales, Keynsham

Printing inks supplied by Shackell Edwards

Printed at the New Chapter Press by Alan Jenkins and Colin Costello on Harris-Aurelia and Falcon presses

Bound at the Pitman Press, Bath

Contents

Acknowledgements

I wish to express my deepest gratitude and thanks to Kenneth and Mabel Selfe for granting me access and exclusive rights to the Short family collection of 19th Century New Forest Photographs, and to Sylvia Puckett, niece of 'Brusher' Mills for providing background information.

To Mike Wicks for his enthusiasm and invaluable editorial assistance in the production of this book and to Alan Cameron for its overall typography and design. To Neil Hargett for his support and encouragement during the three years' preparation of this book and finally to the New Forest itself for becoming 900 years of age.

Mike Walford
1979

EG Short
1881

Lyndhurst ~ capital of the New Forest

Lyndhurst was mentioned in the Domesday Book as a Royal Manor, the name implying 'a wood of lime trees', but curiously, nowadays no limes are to be seen. What is certain, is that Lyndhurst's central location makes it an excellent base for visitors wishing to explore and enjoy the flora and fauna of the New Forest. Travel in any direction and one encounters an enormous variety of plant, tree and animal life.

Perhaps the main architectural attraction of the town is the church. Erected in 1860–1 on an artificial mound, the building is dedicated to St. Michael and supercedes a former building on the same site. The building is constructed of local brick with Bathstone dressings with Purbeck marble columns forming the chancel arch. But the most prized asset of St. Michael's is a magnificent fresco by Lord Frederick Leighton.

Lord Leighton was an artist of some repute, knighted in 1878, created baronet in 1886, then Baron Leighton of Stretton in 1896. He was Lieutenant-colonel of the 20th Middlesex (Artists') Rifle Volunteers and Honorary Colonel, and holder, of the Volunteer Decoration. He was made Commander of the Legion of Honour in 1889, Commander of the Order of Leopold and Knight of the Prussian Order 'pour le merite'.

Leighton's painting was influenced by the Italian ideals and the styles of

Lyndhurst High Street viewed from the main Southampton road

Grotteschi, Raphael and Angelo. He made his first real impact in 1855, when his painting *Cimabue's Madonna carried in procession through the streets of Florence* startled the Royal Academy. He was then twenty-five years old and living and painting in Rome. After Leighton's initial impact on the public he was acclaimed throughout Europe receiving many accolades and in later years becoming President of the Royal Academy.

But before Leighton achieved artistic recognition, he volunteered to conduct an experiment on the blank eastern wall of St. Michael's. At this period, fresco painting was considered impractical in England, because of our very humid climate. Leighton chose to paint his picture with the medium of water-glass, with which he sought to give the painting permanence by the infusion of liquid flint.

From the first preparation of the wall to the last splashes of colour, liquid flint, a medium of wax, resin, oil of lavender and artist's copal was used. The colours were all ground up in these solutions and the composition diluted in

Below **The Fox and Hounds in the High Street**
Opposite **St. Michael's Church and the Queen's House**

twice the bulk of rectified spirits of turpentine, this formed a liquid with which the pores of the wall were thoroughly saturated. A firm, solid mass was thus obtained on the evaporation of the volatile oils.

The subject portrayed is *The Parable of the Wise and Foolish Virgins,* fifteen figures of life size proportions with several attendants occupying an area twenty-four feet long by eight feet high to cover the whole of the wall space beneath the eastern window of the church.

As well as the fresco the church also has a superb collection of Pre-Raphaelite windows. Lord Leighton brought down to Lyndhurst some of that famous collection of artists, the Pre-Raphaelite Brotherhood, which was formed in 1848 by Holman Hunt to 'present on canvas what was seen through nature'. Dante Gabriel Rossetti, Ford Maddox Browne and Sir Edward Burne Jones all contributed to the church as it is seen today.

The east window, sited above the Leighton fresco, was designed by Burne Jones in 1862 and represents *The New Jerusalem.* He was also responsible for the south transept window completed in 1863. This is split into four sections, depicting - Joshua at the battle of Ajalon; Elijah praying on Mount Carmel for

Lord Leighton's Fresco

Lord Frederick Leighton

fire from heaven to defeat the prophets of Baal; Saint Stephen being stoned and Saint Peter being delivered from prison. Rossetti added the two angels to the upper tracery off this window.

The north transept window, designed by Clayton and Bell, is called the 'Te Deum' window and illustrates the four lines in the canticle of that name. The west window was designed by Charles Kemp in 1903 and depicts the archangels, Gabriel, Uriel, Raphael and Michael.

Another interesting feature is the church clock, made by Cooke of York in 1868. This is an eight-day turret clock, comprised of three dials, each seven feet in diameter. It is unusual in having both a gravity escapement and a remontaire and is considered to be an outstanding example of its kind.

The coat-of-arms and crest over the west door belonged to the Chevalier de

Lord Frederick Leighton

Mr & Mrs Gladstone on holiday in Lyndhurst

Chatelain who translated the works of Shakespeare into french. He lived in Lyndhurst for many years and his wife is buried near the west door. Also buried in the churchyard is Mrs. Reginald Hargreaves, whose maiden name was Alice Liddell. Lewis Carrol used her as the model and subject in his most famous of books, *Alice in Wonderland* and *Alice through the Looking Glass*. The Hargreaves family owned 'Cuffnells', (now demolished) which had a long, stone passage leading to the servants' quarters in the basement. It is reputed that this passage gave Carrol the idea of The White Rabbit scuttling into the hole in the ground.

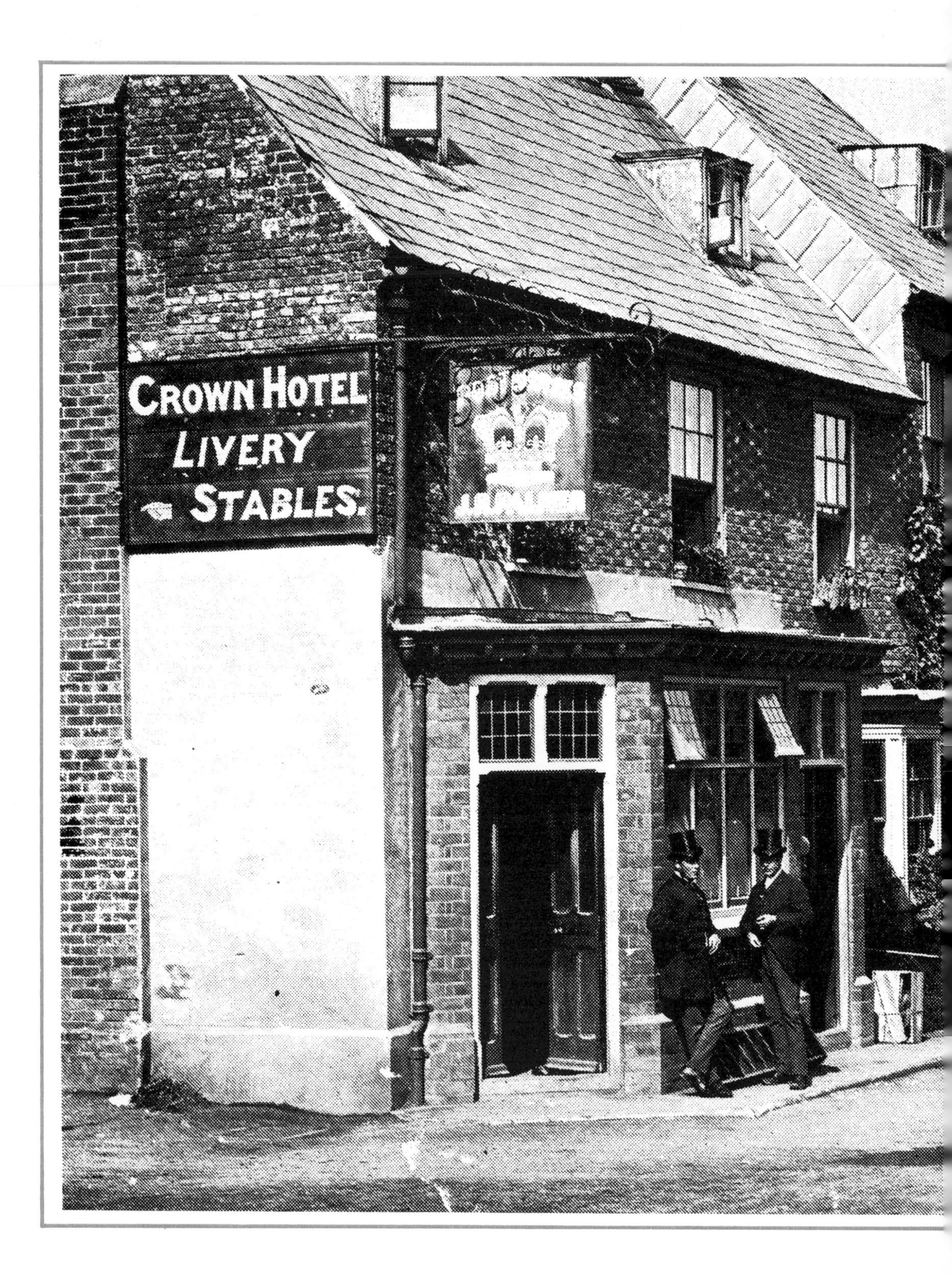
CROWN HOTEL
LIVERY
STABLES.

The original Crown Hotel before being rebuilt in 1897 in a mock Tudor style

The Fox and Hounds where stagecoach passengers were allowed to alight for lunch and liquid refreshment. One old local character nicknamed 'Ol Jack' would perform a funny little tap dance and collect pennies whilst still dancing.

It is at Lyndhurst that the Ancient Court of Verderers preside at regular intervals to attend to their duties as guardians and protectors of Forest Laws. Forest interests are protected against civil and private encroachments to ensure that the common rights of the foresters are maintained.

Forest rights date back to 1016, when King Canute passed an act granting freemen rights 'in Vert and Venison' outside of the Royal Chase. William the Conqueror, an avid hunter, made the Forest his own Royal Hunting Ground and severe penalties were imposed on foresters poaching deer or enclosing land. To enable commoners to continue to eke out their humble existence, he granted them the right to gather fuel and to turn out their own cattle and horses to pasture freely. These laws established the 'commoners' rights' which persist to the present day.

These commoners' rights were —

The Rights of Turbary - which permitted commoners to cut turves or peat from the heath for fuel. The turves were cut yearly to a set pattern of cut one turf and leave two, this enabled turves to grow in a three-year cycle. The size of turf was limited to 9″ x 18″ and the twelve hundred cottages which were erected before the reign of Elizabeth I each had the right to collect four thousand turves every year. There was a fee paid of sixpence for one thousand turves, this was known as 'smoke money'.

The Rights of Pannage or Mast - this allowed pigs to graze in the Forest from 25 September until 22 November each year. Pigs were, and still are, released into the Forest to root out and feast on fallen acorns and beechnuts. Not only were the pigs fattened for the benefit of their owners at Christmas but they also prevented grazing cattle and horses from consuming vast amounts of green, unripened acorns, causing stomach inflammation and possible death.

The Rights of Estover which related to the collection of wood from the Forest. Wood was cut and assigned to certain houses for collection by the cartload. The wood was measured in *cords,* bundles eight feet long by four deep and four high. Sizable timber was sold to city merchants and the branches and sticks were used for fuel and a host of country crafts.

The Rights of Common Pasture which applied to the grazing of ponies, donkeys and cattle, were exercised from 22 November when the cattle were rounded-up and brought into their owners' enclosures until 4 May. This was known as 'winter heyning'. The period 20 June until 20 July was the 'summer-fence' when they were rounded-up again to allow the deer hunts to run without hindrance. In 1877 the fencing was done away with and the animals were allowed to graze the whole year round.

Verderers have the authority to regulate the standard and number of stallions on the Forest to improve the vigour of the stock. They also organise the highly colourful 'pony drifts' which are round-ups or drives. Auctions are held for the sale of the ponies, ownership being determined by brands. The pony sales are still very much part of Forest life, the annual sales taking place at Beaulieu Road Station.

The Rights of Common or Marl - 'marl' is a mixture of carbonate of lime and clay and was used as a compost for gardening purposes. The heathlands of the Forest are very acid and the addition of the chalky marl neutralised and improved the soil structure.

The Fern Collectors

Fern Rights - fern collection took place after 29 September each year, the ferns being harvested for use as litter. Cutting was not permitted before that date as until then the fern's sap was in full flow and cutting would have bled the plants to death. Tickets were issued to commoners for a certain number of loads, fern litter being sold by the wagon load.

The Verderers Court

In a similar way, holly-cutting for retail to city traders at Christmas time started at the end of November and for two whole weeks woodsmen lopped-off the tops of the holly trees and the commoner with 'right of access' purchased fixed quotas cut up into 'holly faggots'. Heather collections took place in autumn after the main nectar flow. Apart from the lucrative and delicious heather honey, the actual heather was used to make mats, skeps and in the preparation of cosmetics.

To ensure that all these rights were observed and that payment was made to the Crown, the Verderers appointed *Agisters* or marksmen. Most of the revenue came from the pasture of cattle and ponies, every beast being marked by an Agister, unmarked animals being likely to be impounded and the owner fined.

It should be noted that the New Forest area is remarkable in that in most parts of the United Kingdom animals were fenced in, whereas in the New Forest they were fenced out.

The rights of pannage, turbary and grazing were issued to properties rather than to individuals and rights were retained by the cottage despite changes in ownership. These rights belonged to the chimney and hearth stone of the cottage and where property and cottages fell into decay, in some cases a fireplace only was left intact in a field to maintain these rights. The rights of commoners exist to the present day and many of the old cottages have kept their fire hearths in order to retain rights of peat cutting and gathering of fuel.

The Verderer's Court presides under the Royal Coat of Arms of Charles I adjoining the Queen's House. After the Court Clerk has called for order, the Senior Agister begins the proceedings by stating aloud, 'Oyez, Oyez, Oyez! All manner of persons who have any presentment or matter of thing to do at this Court of Swain-Mote, let him come forward and he shall be herald - God save the Queen.'

The Anglo-Saxon word *swain-mote* is derived from *swain* - freeholder, *mote* - meeting. The Court Verderers are elected by the commoners, on condition that the Verderer owns seventy, or more, acres of land and that each acre of his holding has common rights attached to it. One Verderer is appointed by the Crown to look after Crown interests. The symbol of office of the Verderer is the axe.

In addition to Verderers, there were other important appointments. The Keepers of the Forest were the 'all foresters' and their function was to watch over 'vert and venison' and prevent violation of the Forest laws. (*Vert* is french for green.) Their symbol of office was a horn and each forester was responsible for his 'walk' of the Forest. The Forest was sub-divided into walks and their locations are still indicated on the Ordnance Map of today.

The Woodwards were the woodmen who felled the trees, attended to tree

Hampshire Hogs

surgery, replanted, removed dead wood and undergrowth and maintained the general upkeep and well-being of the Forest. Their symbol of office was the bill-hook.

The Haywards or 'rangers' were appointed to attend to the *purlieus* (boundaries) and fences of commoners adjacent to the Forest and ensured that cattle did not stray to Forest perimeters. Any strays were rounded-up, impounded or returned to the Forest.

The officers mentioned above could bring miscreants before the Court of Swain-mote for the following offences. *Assarting* - to make barren or plain by rooting-up trees and shrubs and by breaking-up for tillage the ground on which the trees had stood. *Purpresture* - enclosure or encroachment without permission, i.e. by building a cottage, fencing-in of common land etc. *Wastage* - laying waste by felling timber, differing from assart, in that the ground was not broken for tillage.

Evidence of a further curious legal custom is to be found in the Verderers' Court. This is 'Rufus' Stirrup Iron' which is a stirrup measuring 10½" x 7½", through which all forest dogs had to pass to escape the practice of 'lawing'. This was designed, during the reign of Henry III, to prevent dogs from savaging the King's deer.

If any dog was not small enough to pass through the stirrup, three claws were cut off each of its fore-paws thus rendering deer safe from attack.

John and Elizabeth Short

The Short family of Lyndhurst

Three members of the Short family of Lyndhurst were well-known in their respective fields. Frederick Golden Short is probably best known for his masterly oil painting of New Forest scenes, whereas his parents were more widely acclaimed for their works of photographic portraiture.

Frederick Short was born in Lyndhurst in 1863, his parents, John and Elizabeth, were both prominent local residents. John Short owned the local chemist shop and he and his wife shared a great interest in photography often exhibiting their work. Elizabeth successfully specialised in portraiture, obtaining a First Class Silver Medal and Certificate of Honour for her work at the Hampshire Loan Exhibition of 1866. Her Majesty, Queen Victoria granted her royal patronage.

Not only was John Short skilled at taking photographs but his expertise as a chemist enabled him to develop the plates and make the prints. It was possibly his mastery of these techniques which ensured that he was granted a monopoly of photographing views of the Exhibition mentioned above.

Among their patrons were Prime Minister and Mrs Gladstone; Lord Leighton PRA; The Right Honourable W. Harcourt MP and many of the young crowned princes of Europe.

LYNDHURST.

JOHN G. SHORT,

DISPENSING CHEMIST, &c.

PHYSICIANS' PRESCRIPTIONS CAREFULLY PREPARED.

GENUINE DRUGS AND CHEMICALS.

PATENT MEDICINES AND PERFUMERY.

TOILET REQUISITES. MEDICATED LOZENGES OF ALL KINDS.

Horse and Cattle Medicines.

SALAD, SPERM, COLZA, AND OTHER OILS, &c., &c.

A Large Assortment of STATIONERY always on Hand.

PHOTOGRAPHS OF THE NEW FOREST,

And also of Sir Frederick Leighton's (P.R.A.) Magnificent Fresco of "The Ten Virgins," in Lyndhurst Church.

An Edition of "The New Forest Handbook," Illustrated, with Ten Choice Cabinet Photographs, Price 10s. 6d.

Albums with Forest Photographs from 2 to 5 Guineas, for Presents.

Under the Patronage of Her Majesty and the Royal Family.

PRIZE MEDAL AND CERTIFICATE OF HONOUR FOR PHOTOGRAPHS OF CHILDREN.

STUDIO OPEN DAILY FOR ALL KINDS OF PORTRAITURE.

N.B.—A complete Series of Beautifully-coloured Glass Transparencies of the New Forest has just been completed, and are shown as Dissolving Views 20 feet in diameter; and a graphic and interesting Lecture, given by Mr. C. J. PHILLIPS, author of "The New Forest Handbook," with Vocal and Pianoforte Illustrations, now Ready.

Managers and Secretaries of Institutions are requested to apply for Terms to J. G. SHORT, LYNDHURST, or to C. J. PHILLIPS, BEDFORD PLACE, SOUTHAMPTON.

Above **Alfred, John (father) and Frederick Short**

Left and Opposite **Notices advertising the services of the Short family**

BRAMSHAW

BOYS' SCHOOL.

ON

WEDNESDAY, Feb. 15, 1882,

MR. F. G. SHORT

WILL GIVE HIS DISSOLVING VIEWS OF

THE NEW FOREST

By the aid of a pair of powerful Oxy-Hydrogen Lime-Light Lanterns, concluding with new Statuary Slides and novel Dissolving effects.

The VIEWS will be accompanied by Pianoforte and Vocal selections.

To COMMENCE at SEVEN o'clock p.m.

ADMISSION:

Reserved Seats, 2s.; Front Seats, 1s.; Back Seats, 6d.

TICKETS to be obtained of Mr. DOMONEY, and at the POST OFFICE, Bramshaw.

N.B.—The proceeds to be handed to Mr. BASSETT in recognition of services to Bramshaw Literary Institute.

Often John and Elizabeth were called upon to give lectures on the New Forest, illustrated by their own photo-slides. Their son, Frederick, who was a student at Southampton College of Art at that time, hand-tinted the glass gelatine plates with great dexterity. When the plates had been coloured, they were projected on to a screen using a Stewardis Bi-Unial Oxy-Hydrogen Lantern with lime-light dissolving views giving an image twenty feet wide by eight deep. The effect on their audiences was stunning!

Frederick continued these shows long after his parents' deaths, to an accompaniment of songs and piano music performed by his sister, Emily, a talented musician.

It is sad to record that of the several hundred gelatine plates, which made up what was once a vast and unique record of our New Forest heritage, only a few have been traced.

Some years later, Frederick's sister-in-law sold the High Street studio, prior to moving to London, and most of the plates were smashed and disposed of. The few that remain are the originals which form the basic collection of illustrations in this book: many are unpublished but some were printed by the author, as postcards, in 1976.

Mabel Short, niece of Frederick Golden Short recalls:

> 'Elizabeth had many distinguished sitters in her neat and unpretending studio. In those days it was quite the fashion to be photographed by her and her works were sent all over Europe.
>
> I do think Grandma Elizabeth must have been a very delightful, clever woman who combined raising a family with her wonderful talent for photography. It is sad that she died so young.
>
> I remember Aunt Emily telling me that Grandma Lizzie was very superstitious and a few days before she died, someone brought some peacock's feathers into the house, which upset her very much. She asked for them to be removed from the house immediately.
>
> As a child, I spent my holidays with Uncle Fred and Aunt Emily and one day, in 1912, Frederick's great friend, Sir Hubert von Herkomer and his wife, Lady Herkomer, came to lunch. There were a comely and pleasant pair. I remember Uncle Fred telling von Herkomer, "my niece, Mabel, wants to become an artist!" He patted my shoulder and replied, "Then you're a lucky girl; you should be very happy". At the time I remember wondering what on earth he meant, but later in life I understood perfectly well. The majority of painters and writers are happy people, perhaps selfishly so!
>
> When my Aunt Emily (Frederick's sister) was young, "Madam" Herkomer gave her piano lessons. She would have been Hubert

Frederick Golden Short in his studio

St. Michael's Church and The Queen's House

Herkomer's mother, I think. Aunt Emily became a clever and delightful pianist but only acquired her great skill through practising for hours upon hours each day.

Herkomer was a true friend of long standing and I have a portrait of Uncle Fred painted by him in 1912. The portrait has been on exhibition in art galleries throughout the South and is still in my possession.

During the 1914-18 War, the Canadians were at Emery Down felling trees and I was staying with Fred and Emily at the Studio in the High Street, opposite the "Fox", and of course, these bronzed, handsome men who called for "a pint" most days did not go unnoticed by us girls. They loved Fred's Forest paintings and he used to cycle up to Emery Down to paint them actually at work. I wonder how many men took back to Canada oil paintings by him? Quite a good number, I guess!'

Frederick Short loved the Forest and was loathe to leave it long. He visited London and Northern England during the late 1880s and made painting trips to Cornwall. Sketches by him of views in the Mediterranean exist, suggesting trips abroad.

Spending most of his time in Lyndhurst, knowing and loving the forest in all its moods and seasons, Golden Short portrayed the local scenery with a truth and understanding that has not been surpassed by any other artist within the Forest. He was a familiar figure, with his paint-box and easel strapped over his shoulder, cycling along the lanes seeking fresh subject matter to work on.

As a member of Southampton Art Society, he was on various committees and a constant exhibitor for many years, his work often attracting particular attention, some of his paintings being sent to the Royal Academy and leading London exhibitions. He had a great zest for life and, although never marrying, had many female friends. His love of music and accomplishment as a musician, led to many musical evenings with friends — musical free-for-alls in his studio.

Some of the paintings by Frederick Short from scenes in the New Forest

Engravings from
'Autumnal Leaves'
by
F. G. Short

Along with his musical ability, he was known for his humour and pranks. On one occasion, when he was returning home with his father and brother, Alfred, after enjoying a pint or two at the Mailman's Arms, they spotted a donkey wandering down the High Street. Seeing that one of the locals had parked his van outside the pub, they opened it up and catching hold of the donkey locked the unfortunate beast inside. Imagine the drinker's face when he opened his van! On another occasion he entered the Lyndhurst Carnival dressed as a butterfly collector, with an attractive young lady ensnared in a huge net slung over his shoulder.

On another occasion, Mabel Short attended the fair at Swan Green with her mother, Fred and Emily. On one of the stalls gypsies were selling small pipes filled with water which young boys would blow over young girls. Emily and Mabel were amazed to see Fred indulging in this childish pastime which he appeared to enjoy very much. Mabel's mother and Emily were quite cross and scolded him for behaving like a small boy. He laughed and replied that he was only doing what the other small boys were doing!

On the more serious side, Fred gave lessons and instructed on the piano. For many years he was the organist at the local Baptist Chapel. The original drawings illustrating *Autumnal Leaves*, a much acclaimed publication of the New Forest, were by him and were reproduced in *The Illustrated London News* of December 1881; he was only nineteen years of age at that time.

The brewers, Strongs of Romsey, commissioned him to paint ten inn signs for £10.00 each, these included: The Bell at Brook; The Fighting Cocks of Godshill; The Forest Inn at Ashurst and The Fox and Hounds at Lyndhurst. Two of these signs are illustrated in this book from the rough proof copy oil paintings.

He was acknowledged by the national press as a young artist 'imbued with the spirit of the woods'. His great friend, Hubert von Herkomer RA, said of his work, 'he had the whole field to himself'.

Frederick Golden Short died in Lyndhurst on 29 July 1936, having spent his entire life in the New Forest. During his lifetime he helped in the struggle to preserve the Forest gaining some partial success. Since his death, his works have become collectors items and very difficult to come by, however, several of his paintings may be seen at Southampton Art Gallery.

Nine hundred years

1079 — William the Conqueror ordered the afforestation of the New Forest. Old laws of the Forest whereby a freeman was entitled to take 'vert and venison' were changed. William proclaimed the Forest his Royal Hunting Ground and to enable the Foresters to make a living, the rights of the 'Commoner' were established.

1273 — The Forest boundaries were extended from Southampton Water in the east to the River Avon in the west. The Forest encroached into Wiltshire in the north and to the Solent and English Channel in the south.

1483 — The Enclosure Act passed by Edward IV stated that when Forest Woods were cleared, they should be enclosed by means of a ditch and a bank. The bank was to be planted with fast-growing thorn hedgerows for a seven year period to allow young, freshly planted saplings of oak and beech within the enclosed areas a chance to grow and establish themselves.

This important Act helped change the forest from a hunting ground to establish itself as a timber production area. From the seeds of young oaks, grew mighty timbers that were used by our Navies for building those mighty galleons that shaped the British Empire in the centuries to follow.

1662 — Charles II legislated to increase the New Forest area to the size it is today. In 1669 he ordered that 400 acres were to be set aside for oaks as by this time the Forest was being depleted of its woods. However the destruction continued at an alarming rate until —

1698 — when legislation was passed to plant 6,000 acres of the Forest but in 1703 a hurricane destroyed 4,000 of the Forest's great oaks. They were not replaced. Meanwhile, the Forest slowly crept steadily towards depletion.

1808 — Many trees were planted and a Forest 'blueprint' was drafted to ensure that felled trees were replaced by new saplings.

1848 — 'Commoners' Rights' were clearly defined.

1851 — The Enclosure Act was passed to enclose a further 10,000 acres.

Denny Wood

Oak in Queen's Bower Wood

Knightwood Oak

Mark Ash, Boldrewood

1854 — A Commission was appointed to overlord and uphold 'Commoners' Priveleges' which were constantly in dispute between 'Swain-Mote' and those 'commoners' demanding their rights.

1877 — The New Forest Act was passed upholding all previous Acts and it was defined that the ancient woodlands of the Forest be hitherto preserved for the benefit of future generations.

1923 — The New Forest was transferred to the Forestry Commission.

1949 — An Act was passed to establish an electoral list of lands entitled to 'rights of common'. Enclosures of land up to 5,000 acres were authorised for timber planting and regeneration of existing wooded areas.

1964 — The fencing of the New Forest was allowed and designated amenity areas were established.

Gritenham Wood

King and Queen Oak, Boldrewood

Queen's Bower Wood

1979 — The 900th Anniversary of the New Forest celebrated by the visit of Her Majesty the Queen and His Royal Highness the Duke of Edinburgh on 12th April 1979. The Royal party visited the Knightwood oak and planted the 'Queen's Oak' nearby mark the occasion.

THE WALKS

Certain parts of the Forest are enclosed by fences, through which the public is allowed access, providing local regulations are observed. These 'rights of way' are called walks. The woods are known as enclosures.

Vinney Ridge — an ornamental ride flanked on either side with conifers, thujas and rhododendrons. These were planted around 1850.

Matley Wood — an old wood of oaks and birch trees on higher ground leading down to the alder thickets that form Matley Bog. The roots of alder trees create and increase the bog grounds.

Wood Fidley — Wood of free grown beeches, near Brockenhurst Railway Lodge.

Ridley Wood — Lovely old wood of pollarded beeches, planted in the sixteenth century. Once reputably a smugglers' meeting place for trading with the 'foresters'. The Royal Oak at Fritham and the Cat and Fiddle were involved in this clandestine trade.

Oakley Wood — Planted in 1853, comprised of oak and scots pine.

New Park — Originally the Old Park dates from 1291.
Protected by Charles II in 1670 for preserving his newly-imported red deer.

Mark Ash Wood — A mixture of free-grown pollarded beeches with undergrowths of holly and thorn.

Highland Water Enclosure — Planted 1869.

Holmsley Water Enclosure — Planted 1811.

Hinchlesdsley Wood — Domesday entry: 'Wislac held half a hide in Hincelveslei'; and it was assessed at that quantity. It is now in the Forest. There is land for two ploughs. It was worth 20 shillings!

Knightwood Oak — Fine pollarded oak and beeches. One of the oldest pollarded Forest trees stands here.

Bushy Bratley — Fine old wood to the east of Ringwood and Cadham.

Queen Bower Wood — Old oaks near New Park.

Setley Plain — A gravelly expanse of heather and furze between Brockenhurst and Lymington.

A midnight courtship in The New Forest

SOME TREES OF THE FOREST

The woods of the New Forest were used for a great variety of commercial and craft purposes but their major use was shipbuilding. The great oaks of the Forest went into the building of those 'great men-of-war' that hunted and ultimately defeated the mighty Spanish and French fleets, thus establishing our British Empire. Many of these great ships were built at Bucklers Hand near Beaulieu.

The other types of wood grown in the Forest were put to numerous different uses—

Alder — good wood to withstand temperature variations. Used on hat blocks, clogs, turnery, butter boards.

Holly and Lime — good carving woods.

Beech — excellent for furniture makers.

Chestnut — used for fences, poles and gates.

Ash — wheelwrights' wood, used on the rims of wheels and carts.

Hazel — wattle hurdles, baskets, trugs and fish traps.

Larch — fences, gates and boatbuilding (i.e. planking).

Beech and Oak — all types of building uses. The surplus wood was used for charcoal burning. The shavings and sawdust of oak is the best fuel material for curing bacon. Beech is best known for butchers' blocks and piano frames.

Scots Pine — pit props, poles, masts, paper pulp.

Spruce — masts, toys and musical instruments.

Walnut — cabinet making, furniture and veneers.

Willow — cricket bats, paddles, clothes pegs, weaving.

Yew — excellent for longbows.

Birch — brush and broom making. Good wood for smoking mackerel and herrings.

Chestnut — fencing, poles, gates. This wood matures very quickly.

Elm — boatbuilding, garden furniture, canal lockgates.

Pollards

The New Forest is an ancient, ornamental woodland and heathland and in many of the enclosures are trees which are hundreds of years old. Past generations have ensured the longevity of these great proud oaks, beeches and chestnuts by lopping the top branches off – this practice is known as *pollarding.* Trees cut in this fashion tend to produce more vigorous growth, their branches spreading horizontally, forming gnarled, bent and hugely deformed patterns, creating bold visual contrasts against their natural surroundings.

Pollarding was not however undertaken to simply improve the appearance of the trees which are basically an economic crop to be harvested in the same way as any other. Stopping the height of a tree's growth meant that the main limbs were nearer to the ground thus enabling them to be reached more easily and safeguarding them from unnecessary shock and damage when felling or lopping took place. In addition a tree grown in this way produced several sizable branches that were easier to handle than the single great trunk.

The timber from pollarded trees was used mainly by the charcoal burners. Low lying branches obviously spared them the effort and time of climbing up great trunks to selected pieces of wood.

Vinney Ridge

Bratley Wood

Holly tops too were also pollarded to allow branches to spread out near ground level. These branches were to provide deer with a winter food source as well as forming some windbreak protection to the actual woodlands.

Forest cottages

Typical foresters' cottages were constructed of cobbled walls of a mixture of mud, clay and stone, 'puddled-up' with straw, heather and rushes to bind the whole mass together. The roofs were low-slung and thatched. The mud walls of clayey, sandy loam were thoroughly trampled to a porridge-like consistency and 'doffed and bonded' by the mud-waller with a trident and prong. The wall was raised between a framework of boards in low sections about two feet high. This was then allowed to dry out and then the boards were moved up and the procedure repeated at the next level.

The dry-out period took two weeks before the next 'rearing' was applied on top of the first. Walls built in this manner stood well and long, but unfortunately they were often 'raised' by inexperienced mudders using wrong mixes of materials, inedaqute footings, not tempering the loam stuff with heather and general ill-use of the mud-prong; consequently the practice fell into disrepute.

The main advantages of mud-walling or 'cob' techniques were the low material costs and the ready availability of the natural Forest ingredients. Walls constructed in this way withstood the ravages of time and provided coolness in summer and warmth in winter. An outer rough-casting of plaster

Pikes Hill

Swan Green

The Church Track at Emery Down

A young girl trimming up a wooden stake

A typical 'mud-walled' cottage

A well-matured cottage

and pebble-dash weatherproofed the mud walls and provided the rough walls with a smooth finish.

The old craft of mud-walling has now died-out in the Forest and has given way to more conventional (and costly!) building methods. Perhaps some budding entrepreneur would care to revive the craft someday and build a 'mud-walled' cottage as an example of Forest architecture? The idea of turning such a building into a Museum of Rural Crafts for the New Forest has appealed to the author, finance permitting. But would planning and building authorities entertain a 'mud-cottage' project?

After the First World War, wounded servicemen were discharged and for a new start in life were given, for a modest sum, small plots of land to build their own properties. Improvised cottages 'mushroomed up', erected out of old disused railway sleepers, corrugated sheets of metal and planks. My own grandfather was one of these men. His dwelling was called 'The Shack' and while being built, my grandmother, Ethel Snook, carried enormous wood sleepers several miles from Eastleigh on the handlebars of her bike.

Ponies

No one is quite certain how the wild ponies came to inhabit the Forest. Some believe the Romans introduced them, others say they are descended from horses and ponies landed from the wrecked ships of the Spanish Armada. It is probably a fusion of both.

Meet of the deer hounds at Swan Green

Deer hounds

August is the time for rounding up the ponies, when Forest riders herd them into corrals. Once caught and enclosed, the ponies are auctioned off and marked for ownership by four agisters elected by the Verderers' Court. The ponies are marked by – (a) branding, denoting ownership (b) tail cutting, this denotes agister's area of control. Tails were cut to only two lengths but this has now been increased to six cuts.

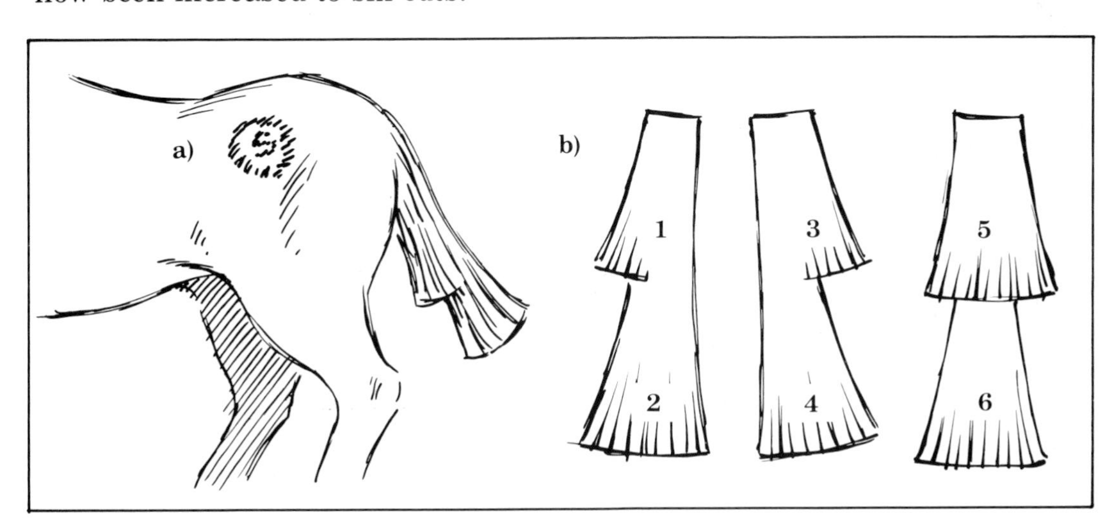

The pony drift ends in autumn and Forest sales are held at Beaulieu Road; organised by the New Forest Pony Breeding and Cattle Society. Once sold and broken in, the ponies make excellent saddle ponies for young children. They were also used to draw governesses' carts, small traps, coster carts and roundsmen's vans. During the spring and summer months, the ponies have a wide area of grass grazing to draw from, whilst in winter their diet changes to holly, gorse and young furze tops.

The donkeys were bred and sold as pit mules to the coal mines and vast numbers were exported in the eighteenth and nineteenth centuries as 'pack mules' to those intrepid pioneers and new frontiersmen of the Americas.

'All Foresters'

'Brusher' Mills

(1838-1905)

Harry 'Brusher' Mills spent most of his life living as a hermit in a cone-shaped hut built out of turf and tree branches within the Forest glades. Harry received his nickname through brushing the local cricket pitch. Being the son of a forester and in his teens, a gardener, his love of outdoor life and the 'lure of the woods' led him to reject the comforts of civilised village life. It is reputed that he never let any person enter his hut and that he slept on a sack stuffed with oak leaves and mosses. This dormouse existence was probably quite cosy.

Around the villages he became a popular attraction, especially to tourists enroute for Bournemouth. The four-in-hand coaches passed regularly through Lyndhurst and couriers would point him out to the passengers. These coaches stopped over on their journeys at the Crown Hotel, Lyndhurst for refreshments and 'Brusher' would quite often be waiting for their arrival. Having a curious audience, he would entertain them all to the spectacle of his snakes housed in two tins slung down from around his shoulders. He handled the snakes with great dexterity and although he extracted the venom, the snakes could still give a vicious bite! 'Brusher' demonstrated how snakes were caught by use of his long-handled fork and then by nipping them with finger and thumb directly behind the head, thus immobilising them. With the use of his scissors,

'Brusher' Mills - celebrated snake catcher

hung around his neck (see photograph) he extracted the venom. His living was made by clearing out snakes' nests from parks, gardens and the Forest itself. Some snakes were sold to Lord Londesborough of Northwood who paid 'Brusher' a fee of one shilling per head for every reptile caught. Londesborough in turn sold them to London Zoological Gardens as the food source for the zoo's Hamadryad (cannibal) snakes. The flesh of surplus adders 'Brusher' sold to local chemists as 'clarified adder's fat', a cure for rheumatics and gout!

Every local knew him as a true forester. Once, when taking out a group of people through the Forest, he spotted the neck of a well-laden hip flask protruding from an unsuspecting victim's pocket upon which he quickly feigned an 'attack' and when offered refreshment for his predicament, he accepted with great thirst and remarkable recovery. Like most foresters, he enjoyed a 'tipple' of the hard stuff!

'Brusher' was very fond of entertaining people with his snakes at local fairs, pony sales and garden fetes and was a great attraction to children, whose company he enjoyed. It was not unknown for him to carry a couple of adders around in his great overcoat pockets and after being encouraged with a glass or two of beer at the local inns, would deposit them on the tables to the horror of some of the more besotten drinkers!

He was a short, stocky figure with great, bushy brows and a face the colour of mahogany. His style of dress was drab to enable him to move unnoticed around the Forest, blending into the background as the snakes basked in the sunshine.

Snake homes are old rat or rabbit burrows and earths of natural formation. At the first rays of sunshine, they leave their holes to bask on bare, sandy strips of soil to gain maximum warmth and solitude. Here 'Brusher' pronged them with his long forked stick on either side of the neck behind the jaw bones. Whereupon he seized them up and popped them into a sailcloth bag. His catches were sold to collectors. He buried dead snakes in a manure heap and when reduced to a white skeleton bone comprising of dozens of small ivory rings, he sold them.

'Brusher' regarded snakes as timid creatures and his advice was, if you did not touch them, they wouldn't touch you. A snake never turned on him and he claimed a snake would travel great distances rather than avoid a meeting with a human being.

He was eventually evicted from his hut as a regulation stated that if a person lived for 21 years or more in the Forest, he could not be evicted. When 'Brusher' had lived there for 20 years, a few months short of the overall time to establish his rightful claim, he was dispossessed by the Crown Authorities who burnt his beloved home down. Some public sympathy for his plight prevailed and he

was offered the opportunity to build another hut in the grounds of Mr. Webley (of revolver fame) but ill health and probably grief took its toll.

He went to live with his sister and died in an outbuilding of the Railway Inn at Brockenhurst where he had earlier had a glass of beer, bread and pickles. His headstone bears a carving of snakes and a hut built in a forest enclave. It has been said he caught 4,000 adders and 30,000 other species of snake during the 21 years he spent in his hut.

His sole possessions were found to be a pocket knife, pistol, watch, the clothes he wore, the tools of his trade and a *squoyle*. A squoyle is a wooden missile, sometimes lead weighted, used for hunting squirrels. It was the Forest custom, on New Year's Day, for the men-folk to go hunting squirrels. The squoyles were hurled through the trees at the prey and the unfortunate victims were baked in clay and heartily devoured.

A Gypsy Queen

Gipples

Probably the least welcome of the visitors to the New Forest were the gypsies or gipples, although some families established themselves quite quickly among the foresters. Pony-trading provided their main livelihood but they also practiced other brands of forest craft. They lived mainly in tents called *benders,* made out of old carpets, turves, clothes and hazel bough support frames. The wealthier few lived in painted wagons or *vardos* which were sometimes quite elaborately decorated, both inside and out. A bed usually stretched across one end of the vardo with a drawer fitted underneath for the children to sleep in. As, and when, the family increased in number, the older members moved outside to sleep in the benders.

The gypsy encampments, deep in the forest glades, were found by other gypsies by means of secret signs, for example twigs with the bark stripped down on one side showed in what direction the camp lay and at crossroads clods of earth were left to indicate the route that should be taken. A bad site where gypsies had been made unwelcome was marked by means of two strips of bark hanging from the twig and crossed twigs with a pointed end revealed a good location.

Once settled into a site, the business began of making-up various wares taken from the natural materials found in the Forest. Hazel, willow and elder

A gypsy camp or 'Kair'

saplings were collected and used in the manufacture of carpet beaters, pegs, baskets and various bric-a-brac. The women-folk made up bee skeps and mats from the heather and lavender bottles from small bunches of lavender intertwined with silk ribbon. Flowers, mosses and coloured stones were collected to adorn the baskets. Then when the products were ready the women donned their dresses and aprons and, accompanied by their children, set off, on foot, to the villages to sell their wares to the local folk.

The children themselves were usually dressed in rags and oddments of clothing collected when *Tips coggling*. They normally had no shoes and those fortunate enough to have a pair, padded them out with rags to avoid discomfort, for they were rarely a good fit. The men-folk had a passion for old military clothing, especially boots, and wore brightly-coloured scarves wound twice around their necks and then knotted. Both the men and women always had their small curved pipes to hand and, if tobacco was not available, shredded oak leaves, dried ferns or coltsfoot would suffice.

Evenings were spent around the camp fire or *yog*. The yog was the centre of their lives and tradition had it that one never ventured between a gypsy and his yog. All cooking was done over the yog, the ingredients being forest game, including the reknowned *hotchi witchi* – hedgehogs baked in clay , and odd vegetables taken from the locals' gardens.

Gypsy weddings were colourful affairs which took place at midnight. All the guests, many coming considerable distances, sat themselves around the yog. The ceremony was then conducted in Romani, the gypsy language, the couple's wrists being slightly cut by a peg-knife and then bound together by a wide, satin ribbon. They were each given a bunch of twigs made up of twigs from different types of tree. These were then thrown one by one into the yog; each twig signifying something for the future. After this they leapt together through the fire and then both waded through a bath of water, completing the marriage vows. A large loaf was then hollowed out and passed around to the guests who each put a wedding gift into the loaf. The feast then began to the accompaniment of music and dancing. The food that was passed around included kebabs, meat loaves, manacle cakes and a honey toffee called *claggum*.

Superstition played an important role in the lives of the gypsies. It was, for example, considered unlucky to soap the face on Good Friday (although they were generally averse to washing at anytime and would wash quickly from old biscuit tins filled with water giving a swift rinse to the hands and face) as, when Christ went on a journey he stopped by a dwelling for a drink of water and received instead a vessel of soap suds thrown into his face by the woman of the house.

Gypsies of the New Forest

When a gypsy died, his widow burnt all his belongings, with the curious exception of his jewellery and money; all his crockery was broken and his beloved vardo burnt. He was buried in a hollowed log, lined with flowers, mosses and ferns and accompanying him on his final journey were his pipe, tobacco and matches. Those given Christian burial had their graves covered in wild flowers, ferns, mosses and candles made from beeswax.

During their lives the women-folk passed down the art of *durrikin*, fortune-telling and predictions, to their daughters. Those fortunate enough to possess a set of Tarot cards made use of their gifts by reading the cards to paying customers at fairs or the villagers in their homes. Palmistry, crystal ball gazing and reading the tea-cups were other derivations of this acquired art.

Today the vardos and benders have both been replaced by chrome caravans and more conventional housing. Other ways of earning a living have been adopted to enable them to continue their independent modes of life in the twentieth century.

Children of The New Forest

A ROMANI GLOSSARY

achin-tans — gypsy encampments
benders — tents made of old carpets, turves and hazel bough supports
chavvies — children
chinning kosts — peg-making
claggum — honey toffee
diklo — a man's coloured scarf
gorgios — local, non gypsy, folk
hotchi-witchi — hedgehog baked in clay
joddakai — a woman's apron
kipsie — basket
patrin — secret sign
rommerin — marriage
smiket — a woman's dress
sweggler — small curved pipe
tips coggling — 'totting'. Collecting other people's throw away goods.
vardo — painted caravan
yog — camp-fire

The Charcoal Burners

Charcoal burning is one of the oldest crafts dating back to the Iron Age. Charcoal has had many uses but its most important application is as a heating agent in the extraction and refining of a variety of metals. Before the advent of coke ovens in the eighteenth century it was much used in our iron and steel industries due to its valuable property of burning at a high, steady temperature with no smoke and little ash. Oak and beech were the woods favoured for charcoal production and both these trees were abundant in the New Forest. A great deal of charcoal was despatched to Christchurch Quay, and then shipped to Cornwall for the tin smelting industry. Charcoal together with sulphur and saltpetre, makes gunpowder and large quantities of only the finest quality were sent to the gunpowder factories, one of which was at Eyeworth near Fritham.

The method used to burn charcoal was as follows. Firstly the bark was removed as this creates too much sulphur if burnt. The wood was then cut into two to three foot lengths and left until summertime when burning proper took place. The basic principle of charcoal burning is to heat to a high temperature whilst excluding sufficient air to prevent actual combustion taking place. All water and wood creosote tars are thus driven out leaving a solid, carbon mass.

Queen Beech

A Charcoal Burner's hut

The whole craft depends on the regulation of draughts; the maximum amount of wood being charred and the minimum burned.

Dry wood burns more rapidly than freshly-felled, green timber so the logs are left from winter to summer. Logs are stacked around a vertical pole in a burning pit. The wood is arranged around the pole sloping toward the centre teepee-wigwam fashion. The logs are lit, covered over with freshly-cut turves and the whole plastered over with wet earth. The centre pole is then removed leaving a pipe-hole into which cold charcoal is dropped followed by twigs, then hot freshly shovelled charcoal. These sandwich layers are repeated until the hole is filled. When copious white smoke shows that combustion is well under way turves are placed over the hole to prevent further draught and the escape of heat. The charcoal burning is now watched by teams around the clock, night and day. If flames break through they are easily extinguished by the application of water and fresh turves. Completion of the process was signalled by any escaping smoke turning from white to blue.

Charcoal burners lived and worked in teams in glades in the Forest, this had several advantages. Team work made observation and attention easier. There were no transportation costs as the raw material, wood, was close at hand. The leafy forest glades of summer provided shelter from wind and rain. However when coal mining began on a more massive scale the old ways of charcoal burning fell in sad decline. In an attempt to complete with coal, huge steel furnaces were built in areas outside the region and mechanised production methods took over.

Carting the logs

The Rufus Stone

The most famous of New Forest charcoal burners was one Purkiss who conveyed the slain body of William Rufus, the Red King of England, to Winchester Cathedral where he was buried.

On August 2nd, A.D. 1100, William II was out hunting deer in the New Forest with his royal entourage, and in the evening his body was found pierced by an arrow. His actual slayer was believed to be Sir Walter Tyrell who fled to France after the event.

Whilst Tyrell was in self-imposed exile, his lands and possessions were left intact and he returned in later years to take up his former residence in England during the reign of Henry I. Was there some intrigue between Tyrell and Henry, or even a group of barons?

William Rufus was the second son of William the Conqueror and his reign was an unpopular one. He was crowned King of the English in 1087; the people rallied to him due to his very strong nature, in the hope of protecting them from the oppressive barons of the period. His elder brother Robert ruled Normandy but was considered by the Conqueror to be too weak to control England. Henry, the third son, had no kingdom.

In 1088 the barons broke into rebellion in the name of William's brother Robert. William mobilised the English to defend his monarchy and the rebellion was finally quelled after the seige of Rochester.

Once the rebellion was over, he turned on baron and peasant alike, gathering around him bands of mercenaries who plundered and preyed on the people. The Church suffered also at his hands and his chief minister, Ranulf Flambard, exacted severe taxes and duties from the whole population.

Charcoal Burning

His death roused no tears and he was buried without ceremony at Winchester Cathedral.

His brother Henry hastened to Winchester on hearing news of his death and was proclaimed King by the barons, who were all at Winchester at the time. At his Westminster coronation he swore to atone for all his brother's evils and became known as the 'Lion of Justice' – a title he lived up to!

The spot where Rufus was slain is at Canterton Glen and it was here that Lord Delaware erected a stone to mark the site in 1745. Due to vandalism and natural erosion, the stone was encased in metal and duly inscribed.

People of the Night

The New Forest with its dense woods, marshes and creeks, gave wonderful cover for the smuggling industries of the seventeenth and eighteenth centuries, and there were many routes through the forest glades for this clandestine trade. Three local inns were well known for harbouring the smugglers. They were the 'Cat and Fiddle', the 'Queen's Head' at Burley, and the 'Royal Oak' at Fritham.

Many forest houses had moveable hearths to hide contraband from the Excise Officers. Another favourite place to conceal the merchandise was under horse stable flagstones. (Smugglers coined the saying 'Keystone under the hearth, keystone under the horse's belly'.) Some of the cottages at Emery Down were used in this manner.

The contraband consisted of silks, lace, spices, brandy, tea, and any fine, quickly saleable product that came to hand. Penalties were severe and those unlucky enough to be caught either dangled at the end of a rope at the famous Hangman's Tree at Mark Way, called the 'Naked Man', or faced deportation to the colonies.

Many Hampshire and Wiltshire gentry sponsored these smuggling operations and whole villages were involved in the trade. Wiltshire folk earned the nickname of 'Moonrakers' when two smugglers were transporting casks of brandy on their donkey to Devizes at night. The donkey, for some reason, bolted and threw the casks into a river. An Excise Officer came upon the two unfortunate smugglers trying to fish out the casks with a rake. The men, seeing the moon's reflection in the water, and hastily trying to cover up for their actions, told the Officer that they were raking for cheese. The Excise man was so convulsed with laughter over two grown men behaving like simpletons by raking the 'shadder of tha moon' thinking it to be cheese, that he spread the tale around the country about the 'fool' Wiltshire folk. They were known thereafter as 'the Moonrakers'.

Taken from an old postcard

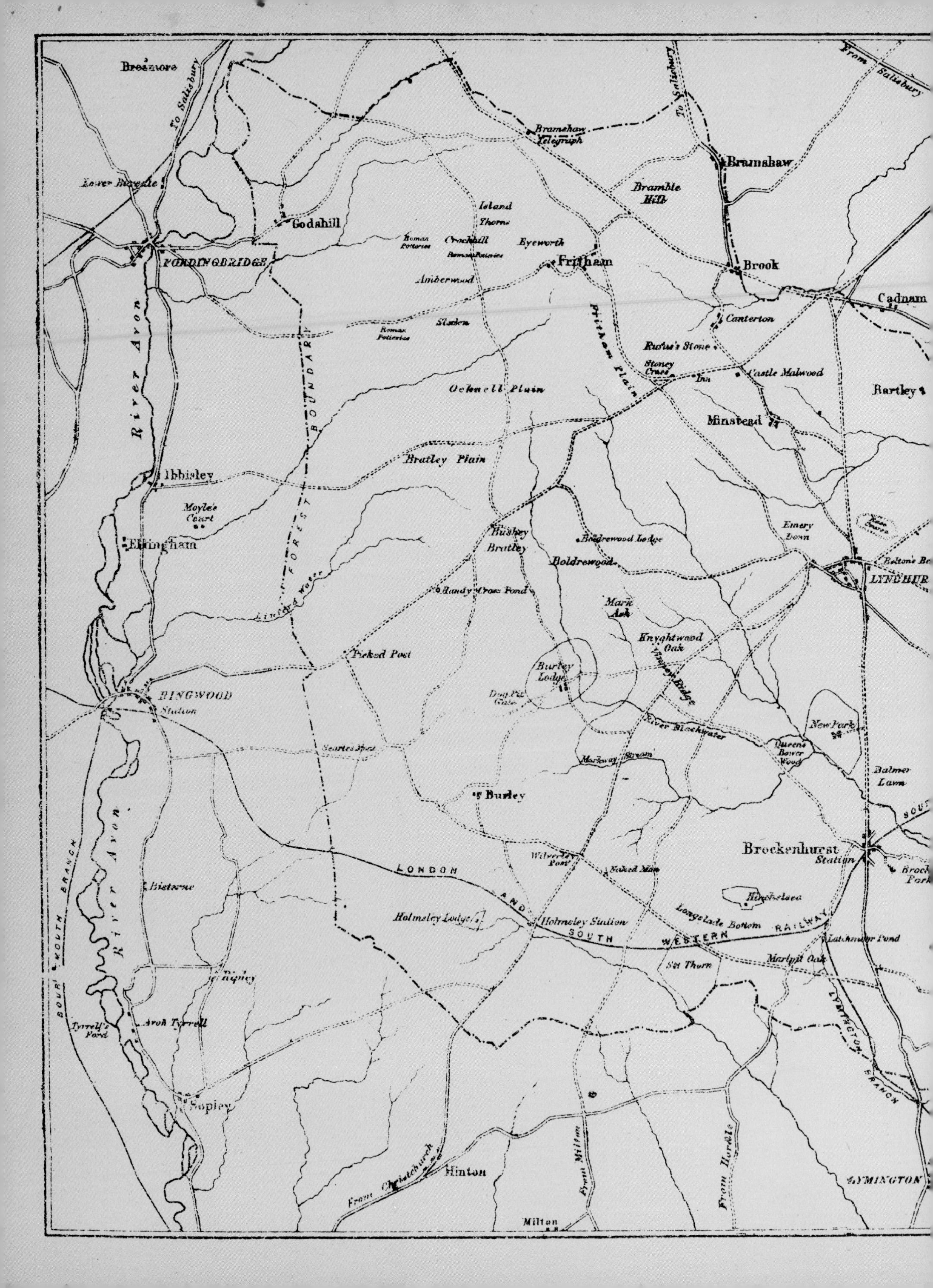

Breamore
To Salisbury
Lower Burgate
Godshill
FORDINGBRIDGE
River Avon
Ibbisley
Moyle's Court
Ellingham
RINGWOOD
Station
Bisterne
Ripley
Avon Tyrrell
Tyrrell's Ford
Sopley
Hinton
From Christchurch
Milton
From Milton
From Hordle
LYMINGTON
Bramshaw Telegraph
Bramshaw
Bramble Hill
Island Thorns
Crockhill
Eyeworth
Fritham
Amberwood
Sloden
Ocknell Plain
Bratley Plain
FOREST BOUNDARY
Fritham Plain
Brook
Cadnam
Canterton
Rufus's Stone
Stoney Cross
Inn
Castle Malwood
Bartley
Minstead
Bushey Bratley
Boldrewood Lodge
Boldrewood
Mark Ash
Knyghtwood Oak
Burley Lodge
Picked Post
Burley
Emery Down
LYNDHUR
New Park
River Blackwater
Balmer Lawn
Brockenhurst
Station
Naked Man
Holmsley Lodge
Holmsley Station
LONDON AND SOUTH WESTERN RAILWAY
Longslade Bottom
Latchmoor Pond
Marlpit Oak
Set Thorn
LYMINGTON BRANCH
SOUTHAMPTON BRANCH
River Avon
From Salisbury